NATURE'S BABIES

NATURE'S BABIES

MIKE DILGER

METRO BOOKS
NEW YORK

To the Browns – an amazing family of naturalists...
and come to think of it, an amazing family as well.

This 2008 edition published by Metro Books,
by arrangement with HarperCollins Publishers Ltd.

Metro Books
122 Fifth Avenue
New York, NY 10011

ISBN-13: 978-1-4351-1135-6

Printed and bound in China

10 9 8 7 6 5 4 3 2 1

CONTENTS

INTRODUCTION

Nature's Babies is an unashamed celebration of the fully technicoloured glory of the natural world itself. The seemingly infinite variety of different baby shapes and sizes is of course down to the cleverest and most powerful beast of them all: evolution. What else would have created babies that at one end of the spectrum are impossibly cute, yet at the other end would not look out of place in the most off-the-wall science fiction novels?

Parenting skills can vary enormously from the non-existent to the lavish. For some animals being born is a rude awakening into a harsh, unforgiving world with no parental care whatsoever – just ask leatherback turtle hatchlings as they have to run the gauntlet to sea!

This book showcases some of the weirdest and wonderful stories of the babies' development, too. Who would have thought, for example, that a grey kangaroo's baby is born no larger than a kidney bean, and from the moment it enters the world has the most daunting journey to complete even before it will be able to feed for the first time? And exactly why do Galápagos tortoises take an astonishingly long 25 years to reach maturity?

Whilst focusing on the babies, this book will hopefully also test our own notions of how we humans fit into the natural world. We think of our birth, babyhood and adolescence as normal, but how 'normal' compared to other animals are we? Whilst we perhaps arrogantly think of the human race as producing model babies and parental skills that are unsurpassed, do we in fact have something to learn from our wild cousins? After reading *Nature's Babies*, you decide!

LITTLE GRIZZLIES

Found right across North America, Europe and Russia, with smaller pockets in Asia, the brown bear is both the most common and widespread of all eight bear species. The famed grizzly is the race of brown bear most commonly found in Alaska and Canada, so-called because its hair is lighter at the tip than at the base which gives this bear a 'grizzled' appearance.

The larger grizzlies can reach an impressive 700 kg (1,500 lb) in weight, and with their massive shoulders, huge forearms and plate-sized paws, they must be one of the strongest animals in the world; their only predator is, of course, man and his gun. Ironically for an animal with such size and strength, the main diet of grizzlies tends to be roots and fungi, supplemented by fish and small mammals if and when available. Their incredible bulk is often used to drive wolves and cougars away from kills.

During times of plenty in the summer months, the female grizzly puts down huge reserves of fat which she relies on to get her through the winter. The breeding season also occurs in the summer, but the fertilized egg will not be implanted and begin to grow until the winter, when the female is tucked away asleep in her den, hidden away from the worst of the weather. The most common litter size is two; the blind, toothless and hairless cubs are born in the winter den and grow quickly on their mother's milk, only emerging with their mother into the big, wide world when spring finally breaks.

Little grizzlies remain with their mother for two to four years, learning the 'tricks of the trade' which will prove essential if they are to grow up as big and strong as their parents.

LIKE A DUCK TO WATER

Unlike seals and dolphins, our smallest marine mammal has no blubber. This means that adult sea otters have to spend up to three hours a day grooming their fur meticulously to ensure that it stays in top condition and remains able to trap the vital insulating layer of air which keeps them warm.

When they are not busy grooming themselves, sea otters spend a large part of the day hunting for food. From depths of up to 40 m (131 ft) they retrieve clams and sea urchins from among the rich kelp forests on the sea floor and bring these up to the surface. The sea otter is an animal which likes to spend a large part of its life belly up, even when feeding. Lying on its back, it uses its underside as a table to crack open these tough shells with the help of a special stone which it retrieves from a 'waistcoat pocket' situated under its armpit.

Although the birth of the single pup takes place on shore, the mother immediately guides it straight into the water. Despite being born with its eyes open, and with a full set of milk-teeth and baby fur, the sea otter pup is initially very vulnerable to the cold, and so it spends the first four weeks of its life being groomed and fed on its mother's belly. When the mother does have to leave her pup on the surface whilst diving for food, she often wraps her youngster up in kelp to prevent it drifting off. As the pup's fur traps so much air, it bobs on the surface like a cork until its mother comes back to retrieve it!

Baby sea otters spend much of their first year of life on their mother's belly, where they are groomed, fed and kept warm.

A LEAP OF FAITH

With its torpedo-shaped body, long, narrow wings and its dagger-like bill, the gannet is a very lean and very mean fishing machine. It is also an incredibly sociable bird during the breeding season and nests in densely packed colonies on steep cliffs and raised slopes around the coasts and islands surrounding Britain, northern Europe and northeast America.

Gannets are usually faithful to both their partner and to their breeding location, and pairs of birds will often return to exactly the same tiny territory of guano-stained rock each year. This special area will be stoutly defended against all neighbours and any newcomers by ritualized displays between the pair. If trespassers don't get the earlier, more subtle messages, they will receive a quick jab of the gannet's sharp bill.

Once the single chick is hatched it is initially guarded around the clock by at least one parent to ensure that it is not snatched by any opportunistic gulls eager for an easy meal. As each adult returns from a fishing mission, the black, naked youngster reaches deep down into its parent's mouth to feed on regurgitated fish. The youngster will grow quickly on this rich diet of mackerel or herring which it is brought by its conscientious parents several times a day. But then, at around 90 days, the parents suddenly stop feeding their offspring in an effort to force it to fledge. Egged on by hunger, the still flightless chick has to make a kamikaze-style jump down to the waters below before it can begin paddling south for the winter. Only once it has lost a bit of weight from such energetic paddling will it finally be able to take to the air and hunt for itself.

A gannet chick waiting to decide whether it is mother (father who has to go and catch breakfast.

PRICKLY YOUNGSTERS

So-called for its fondness for hedgerows and because of a snout that resembles a pig, the hedgehog is very aptly named indeed. Setting aside its preferred habitat and nose, the hedgehog's other most distinguishing feature is, of course, its prickly nature.

During the day hedgehogs will seek shelter in a nest of grass and leaves under bushes or logs until they take their cue from dusk to begin roaming through parks, neighbouring gardens and woods in their perennial search for earthworms, slugs and snails. To prevent themselves actually figuring on the menus of other larger predators such as badgers and foxes, they are famously capable of rolling into a thorny, impenetrable ball to protect their vulnerable undersides.

For obvious reasons, a male wishing to mate with a female has to do so very carefully, and not until she is absolutely ready! As hedgehogs hibernate during the winter, their noisy mating takes place during the summer months and just over a month later four to five youngsters are born. Fortunately for the mother, the baby hedgehogs are 'spine-less' at first, but only a few hours after birth the baby's first set of nearly 150 spines will already have pushed up through the skin. By the twelfth day the youngsters have managed the art of curling up when necessary, and after a further month and a couple of sets of new spines later, the young hedgehogs become perfect miniature replicas of their prickly parents.

hedgehog's prickles, or
ines, are actually hollow
iff hairs that can be raised
t will if danger threatens.

THE LONGEST DROP

It's quite a boast to declare that one is the tallest of all land-living animals, and one which the giraffe is able to make without fear of contradiction. Over thousands of years giraffes have gradually evolved from their shorter-necked ancestors so that today the largest males can reach the dizzying height of 5 m (16 ft) - to the very tips of their horns! The giraffe's height enables it to browse its favourite food of spiny acacia leaves at levels higher than all the other herbivores are capable of reaching.

In addition to an impressive neck, which incidentally only contains the same number of bones as a human neck (seven), the giraffe possesses long, elegant legs which can produce impressive bursts of speed when necessary and also keep hungry lions at bay with powerful kicks.

Female giraffes associate in small groups whilst the males live either in 'bachelor' herds or on their own. The older and larger males tend to mate most of the females in the herd after seeing off any competition through a series of jousts where necks and heads are frequently swung like a wrecking ball-and-chain to assert dominance. The gestation period of the giraffe is long and can last up to 15 months, and the mother gives birth to the single calf standing up. This means that the newborn calf's entry into the world entails it landing with a terrific thud on the ground below. Within just a few hours the world's tallest baby is capable of following its mother. This is absolutely essential; there are so many predators on the prowl that the youngster really does have to hit the ground running!

Even the world's tallest baby has to look up to its mother!

HATCHED IN A HUDDLE

Not only is the Emperor penguin content with being the tallest and heaviest of all living penguins, but it is also the only species tough – or crazy – enough to breed during the Antarctic winter – surely the most challenging environment on earth in which to raise a family.

When temperatures drop to below -40°C (-40°F) and polar winds gust at over 190 km/h (120 mph), the only way that these penguins are able to survive during the breeding season is by being very sociable: they crowd together in large groups and thus protect themselves from the elements. These huddles move constantly so that the birds along the colder edge can eventually shuffle into the middle of the group, thereby temporarily exchanging places with the warmer birds in the centre, who must then take their turn on the chilly periphery.

Emperor penguins stay faithful to their mate each breeding season. After an elaborate courtship, the female lays a single, thick-shelled egg, which is then carefully deposited onto the feet of the male to incubate in a special pouch. She then promptly deserts him for two months to feed out at sea. Together with his fellow abandoned males, the male fasts for the entire 65 days of incubation, until the female arrives back to feed the newly-hatched chick on a rich diet of regurgitated fish, krill and squid. It is only then that the half-starved males are allowed to leave and feed out at sea.

To begin with the young chicks are not well insulated and so they must stay sheltered in their mother's brood pouch for at least 50 days before they join crèches with other youngsters. Here they keep warm by huddling and learning the skills that they will eventually need to survive as breeding adults.

'Brrr! It's cold out there.' A baby Emperor peers out on its icy world.

BRINGING UP BABY

This largest of all living land animals really needs no introduction. With a huge set of ears, a long pair of tusks and a versatile trunk, the African bush elephant is probably the best known and the biggest of all three species of elephant and is also undisputed master of the African savanna.

Female African elephants spend their whole lives in social groups. These consist of the dominant female (matriarch), and an array of immediate family members including mothers, daughters, sisters and aunts. Adult males, on the other hand, lead either solitary lives, or live in loose 'bachelor' herds and only join the female unit when one of the herd is sexually receptive. Females ready to mate will seek out the biggest, strongest and oldest bull elephants: these will be the ones who have already asserted their prowess by fighting with and driving away any other potential suitors.

The elephant's pregnancy is the longest in the natural world and lasts 22 months. At the end of this gestation period, the mother gives birth to a calf weighing up to 120 kg (264 lb). The young elephant is born with very few survival instincts and must therefore rely on its elders to teach it everything it needs to know during a prolonged upbringing. All members of the tight-knit female group participate in the care and protection of the newborn calf and it quickly becomes the centre of attention. Since everyone is related, there is never a shortage of babysitters on hand to help, too!

Baby elephants are never short of willing playmates.

THE BIGGEST CLUTCH

By choosing a flightless lifestyle, the ostrich has been able
to increase its size and weight to such an extent that it is now
the world's largest and heaviest bird. These features, together
with their tremendous eyesight, phenomenal running speed
and a vicious kick, enable them to protect themselves on the
predator-riddled plains of eastern and southern Africa.

In the wild, ostriches are nomadic and will travel long distances
in mixed-sex herds with other grazing animals such as zebra
and antelope to track down the seeds, plant matter and
odd insect which make up their diet. As ostriches lack teeth, they
swallow stones to help grind up these tough foodstuffs in their
gizzard. Although their wings are not used in flight, they are still
large with a wingspan of over 2 m (6 ft 6 in), and male ostriches
use them in elaborate mating displays when they compete for
territory, social status and the all-important attentions of a small
harem of females, or hens.

Once the dominant male has successfully fought off the
competition, he will then mate with all of his females. This
often leads to many of the hens laying their eggs in the same
communal nest, resulting in the production of a clutch of over
30 eggs. Weighing in at 1.5 kg (3 lb 5 oz) each, the world's
heaviest eggs are then incubated by the dominant hen and the
male until they hatch after about 40 days. The father's
responsibilities do not stop there, as he then assumes sole
control of the crèche, in order to both defend the hatchlings and
also teach them what to feed on and how to find it.

Until they are able to fend
or and defend themselves,
ostrich chicks will always
stick to safety in numbers.

JUST A BIG BABY

Surely one of the most celebrated of all beasts among whale-watchers because of their ability to virtually leap clear of the water and their haunting songs, the humpbacks are also thought to carry out the longest migration of any mammal. Each year they will travel from their summer feeding areas in the higher latitudes to breed and give birth in tropical waters during the winter – a round trip of over 16,000 km (10,000 miles).

The humpback is found in all the major oceans and can reach an impressive 12 to 17 m (39 to 55 ft) in length. Their knobbly flippers are immensely long and can be used, together with the colour of the underside of the tail, to identify different individuals. Humpbacks only feed on krill and small shoaling fish in the summer, before living off their fat reserves during the breeding season. When feeding, they are capable of working cooperatively using a technique called 'bubble-netting': a number of whales will drive a shoal of fish into a tight cylinder of underwater bubbles, before piling in, mouth agape, to swallow – in just a few gulps! – thousands of fish filtered from the water by special baleen plates.

The male humpbacks are particularly vocal, and are capable of producing loud and complex 'songs' by forcing air through their nasal cavities. It is not understood if this is used by breeding males to try and intimidate other males or attract females, or even if it serves another function entirely. Groups of males will often compete for the females, and on their return to the tropics twelve months later, the females will give birth to a 5 m (16 ft) long, 700 kg (1,500 lb) calf. The young calf will then be a constant shadow beside its mother until weaned a year later.

The baby humpback will spend at least a year with its mother before drifting off on its own into the big blue yonder.

BORN IN THE FREEZER

Called 'Nanuk of the North' by the Inuit peoples, the polar bear is perfectly adapted for a life on pack-ice, shoreline or the open sea, and being the Arctic's top predator it has nothing to fear except man, his rifle and global warming.

Whilst the polar bears' fur appears a creamy white, the individual hairs are actually hollow and translucent and provide the perfect camouflage whilst they are out on the sea-ice hunting their favoured prey of ringed and bearded seals. To enable the bear to survive the often bitter Arctic weather, it is insulated by a thick layer of fatty blubber and large feet, which act like snow-shoes by spreading the weight whilst it walks across snow or thin ice.

The roving males will mate with a number of females on the sea-ice in April and May, after which the females eat huge quantities of food so as to double their weight in preparation for giving birth and the accompanying fast afterwards. In autumn the pregnant female will then dig a den out of a snow drift and give birth to usually two or three cubs between November and January. Sheltered from the worst of the winter, she will then nurse her young cubs on a diet of fat-rich milk until a much slimmer and very hungry mother emerges from the den with her new family in March or April. The cubs will then be inseparable from their courageous and protective mother until they are weaned after two to three years.

With ice for a pillow, the mother polar bear and its cubs can cope with the worst the Arctic can throw at them.

HITCHHIKING BABIES

Equally happy leaping around in the trees or bounding about on the ground, the ring-tailed lemur is immediately recognized by its trademark long, stripy, and bushy tail. This fantastic tail is coloured with roughly 26 black and white rings; it starts with a white stripe at the body and always ends with a black tuft at the tip. Like all lemurs, the 'ring-tail' is only found on the island of Madagascar, where it makes its home in the deciduous forests in the southwest of this biologically diverse island.

The ring-tail is undoubtedly one of the most sociable of all lemurs. They band together to form troops as they rove over their sizeable territories, foraging for fruits and leaves from trees such as the tamarind, or engaging in a spot of communal sunbathing during warm weather. The number of lemurs in any one troop may be as many as 25, with a well-defined hierarchy of older females who dominate the younger females and the hen-pecked males.

The breeding season occurs from April to June. The female is only able to conceive in a small window of just 48 hours, and following a pregnancy of some 140 days either one or two offspring are born. The baby lemurs cling at first to their mother's underside, but when they are older they climb around to hitch a ride on her back instead. Once they are weaned after five months, the young females remain with their mothers and sisters in the troop, and the ejected and hapless juvenile males try their luck at ingratiating themselves with a neighbouring clan of bossy, domineering females!

Looking more gremlin than lemur, the ring-tailed babies hitch lifts with their mother for at least the first five months of their life.

A LONG CHILDHOOD

The origin of the word 'orang-utan' comes from the Malay and Indonesian words meaning 'person of the forest'. Nothing could more accurately describe these highly intelligent but also gravely threatened close relatives of humans.

Orang-utans are undoubtably the most arboreal of all the great apes: they feed, sleep and even breed in the canopy of their rainforest homes on the islands of Borneo and Sumatra. They are also very solitary creatures, with males and females usually only coming together when they need to mate. Most of an orang-utan's day consists of looking for and eating fruit and other food, and every night it constructs sleeping platforms by weaving branches together.

Females ready to mate will be attracted into the territory of the much larger male by his roaring calls, which are designed to advertise his presence and can carry for great distances through the forest. When the baby orang-utan is born – after a pregnancy which lasts between eight and nine months – it remains inseparable from its mother until it reaches the age of six or seven. The mothers are incredibly patient with their youngsters, who will sleep in their nests until they are weaned at the age of three. The young will still be dependent for a considerable amount of time after weaning as they slowly learn from their teacher the necessary skills to survive on their own. With females living to be about 45 years old and with the interval between births being as long as eight years, it is not surprising that each female will probably have no more than four babies. This is believed the lowest number of any mammal, making each baby orang-utan very special.

The orang-utan babies have much to learn before they finally branch out on their own.

BORN STRIPY

Of all the coats on display in the animal world, none are as distinctive as those of the zebra. The black and white striped pattern of each animal is as unique to each zebra as fingerprints are to each human. Of the three different species of zebra the most common of all is the Plains Zebra, which can be found in the grasslands and savannas of eastern and southern Africa.

Scientists are not entirely sure why zebras are striped. The stripes may help with camouflage and make it more difficult for predators to single out an individual from a running herd, or they may even prevent zebras from being bitten by certain insects. Like most wild horses, Plains Zebras are very sociable and live in small family groups or harems which consist of a resident male stallion with several females and their young. These harems sometimes combine with other groups to form super-herds of thousands, but in spite of the size of these very large herds the family members tend to remain bunched close together.

Female zebras mature earlier than stallions, and a mare may have her first foal by the age of three. From then on the mare will give birth to one foal every twelve months, which she will nurse for up to a year before becoming pregnant again. Just like horses, baby zebras are able to stand, walk and suckle within minutes of being born and – bizarrely – they are brown-striped at birth. During the early part of its life, the vulnerable foal is protected by its mother, the head stallion and other mares who all huddle around it if trouble beckons. If any hungry hyenas or wild dogs come too close, the adult zebras then kick out savagely, so as to keep the foal safe.

Able to stand within minutes of being born, this baby zebra will spend its whole life on the run.

MEERKATS UNITED

Meerkats are celebrated by wildlife film-makers for being among the planet's most engaging animals. These small, charismatic, southern African desert dwellers are, like most of the mongoose family, very sociable animals. If they had a motto it would be 'United we stand, divided we fall', as their whole lives are spent in the company of their own kind in small hyperactive clans of up to 30 individuals.

Meerkats are compulsive burrowers who inhabit large underground networks with multiple entrances. These burrows are occupied at night and vacated during the day when they leave to feed. In addition to their main food group – insects – meerkats will also eat lizards, scorpions, spiders, eggs, small mammals and even occasionally birds. Lunch is located by foraging, whilst one member of the clan stands tall on very effective sentry duty, watching out for any danger. A whistle or bark by the sentry alerts the unaware diners to danger, resulting in a dash for the nearest bolt-hole particularly when their arch enemy, the martial eagle passes over.

The clan consists of a dominant pair who are usually the only couple to mate, their siblings and also their previous offspring. Three pups is a common litter size, and the vulnerable youngsters are kept underground and out of sight until they are at least three weeks old. When finally they emerge into the light, they stay with designated babysitters who will put their own lives at risk when necessary to protect their young charges. Meerkat adults are also excellent teachers, patiently showing their young pupils how to eat venomous scorpions without being stung, a technique that involves carefully removing the stinger first.

Babysitting duties are taken very seriously by the adult members of the meerkat clan.

BIG BROTHER

The ghostly barn owl, a truly cosmopolitan bird, is the most widespread of all owls and is found on all continents apart from Antarctica. These birds happily lodge alongside us in lofts, barns and other outbuildings. To watch an adult barn owl emerge at dusk and quarter the fields and hedgerows in their daily search for mice and voles is an unforgettable experience.

Barn owls have a superb array of tools with which they can catch and kill their prey during even the darkest of nights. Their hearing is incredibly sensitive and any noise is gathered and funnelled into their ear openings by a heart-shaped faces. Any potential rodent prey which has betrayed its general location by sound will be accurately pin-pointed by the owl's phenomenal night vision. Once the rodent has been located the barn owl spirals down silently and lethally, its legs swing forward, and the unfortunate mammal is dispatched by the bird's powerful talons before being swallowed whole.

An established barn owl pair will produce clutches of four to six eggs, and as the eggs hatch at different times, the chicks often resemble a collection of Russian dolls: there is a huge difference in the ages - and therefore the sizes - between the oldest and the youngest chicks. In years when there is plenty of food all the chicks should fledge, but when vole numbers are down, the larger and more dominant chicks will occasionally supplement their diet by swallowing any younger siblings too small to put up any resistance!

In years with abundant role numbers, all the chicks shou survive to fledgling. Only when food is scarce will the youngest chicks have to watch their backs!

PRICELESS BABIES

Black and white rhinos cannot actually be identified by colour, as they are both varying shades of grey. However, the black rhino can be distinguished from its 'white' cousin by being smaller and the rarer of the two in the wild. At the turn of the 20th century, there were hundreds of thousands of black rhino, but illegal poaching for their huge horns has decimated their number and there are now only a few thousand left.

This huge herbivore lives in the grasslands and savannas of southern, eastern and central Africa, where it uses a special prehensile lip to draw fresh twigs and shoots into its mouth. When not browsing for food, the rhino will spend the hottest part of the day either resting in the shade, or wallowing in mud to help keep it cool and offer some protection against skin parasites.

With the exception of mothers and their calves, black rhinos are solitary creatures. They do, however, keep in touch with their neighbouring rhinos by scent-marking with urine and dung. By smelling these 'messages' the rhino can glean a great deal of information, such as letting the local males know when a female is ready to mate. A pregnant female black rhino will carry her baby for 15 to 16 months before giving birth to a single calf weighing around 40 kg (88 lb). Able to follow its mother after just a couple of days, this mini rhino will be inseparable from her for at least two years until it is weaned. During this time, the youngster will have little to fear apart from large packs of hyenas and lions and, of course, man's gun.

This baby rhino will not stray from its mother's side until has bulked up and grown huge horn.

GREEDY GUZZLERS

As grey seals spend at least ten months of the year feeding out in the Atlantic Ocean on a rich diet of fish, the best time to catch up with these gregarious and sociable beasts is when they come ashore to give birth and breed.

The sleek, fat and heavily pregnant females, or cows, are usually the first to come ashore in the autumn at a few special beaches in eastern Canada and northwestern Europe, when they haul themselves up to their favoured pupping spots. The length and breadth of the beach quickly becomes studded with cows who will then all give birth to their furry, white pups within the space of just a few days. Once each cow has bonded with her pup, it is crucial for the pup's survival that it starts suckling without delay. Seal milk is so rich in fat that the youngsters treble their birth rate in the three-week period before they are finally weaned.

Once the mother has fulfilled her responsibilities towards her offspring, she goes off to fraternize with the much larger, resident male bull seal, who has been biding his time to mate with a harem of up to ten females. When all the mating has taken place, both cows and bulls quickly disappear back into the water, leaving the beach behind until the following year.

Before the abandoned pups are able to follow their parents into the sea, they must first shed their baby fur to reveal a sleek, dark, waterproof coat beneath. Only then will they be ready to take on the worst that the north Atlantic can throw at them.

It's 'operation weight gain' for a grey seal pup, as it must treble its weight in just three weeks before being abandoned by its errant mother.

THE FEMININE TOUCH

The bottlenose is the largest of the 'beaked' dolphins, with males reaching a length of 4 m (13 ft). The species is well known for being the star of both the film and television series *Flipper*, and is the species most commonly seen performing in oceanariums all over the world. Bottlenoses can be encountered in every sea and ocean, with the exception of the Polar seas, and they seem to be particularly common along the coasts of numerous islands and continents, which also means that they can often be seen from land at certain well-known viewpoints.

Common bottlenose dolphins live in groups that vary greatly in size, depending on their location; coastal groups usually form pods of between two and fifteen individuals which tend to be smaller than those of their offshore cousins. These pods are made up of related females and their young, which may stay together for many years, and will occasionally be visited by local, amorous adult males. The pod will either forage for fish individually or collectively, and sometimes they can be seen 'fish whacking'. This involves striking fish clean out of the water with their flukes before mopping them up.

When a female in the pod is sexually receptive, the visiting male will often try to restrict her movement before indulging in a whole range of courtship behaviour with her. The male clings to her, poses, strokes her, jaw-clamps and yelps before mating takes place. The young dolphin is born after a pregnancy lasting roughly twelve months and suckles its mother's milk for a further ten to eighteen months. Even when weaned, however, the youngster will continue to associate with its mother for several more years before joining the sisterhood if it is a female, or being banished from the pod if it is a male.

Bottlenose dolphins are renowned for their curiosity and will often approach divers or boats to indulge in spot of 'bow-riding'.

BORN TO CUDDLE

Living high above the treeline in the mountainous areas of central and southern Europe, the 'mountain mouse', or Alpine marmot, is the largest of all the ground squirrels. To ensure survival in this tough environment, the marmots must rely on both their ability to hibernate underground throughout the winter and on their social group working effectively together as a team.

Alpine marmot colonies can be as small as only two or three animals or as large as up to 50, all of whom live together in a series of burrow systems. The colony usually consists of a dominant breeding pair and some of their offspring from previous years. During hibernation the adult marmots cuddle up with the younger individuals, greatly enhancing all their chances of survival. In the spring, marmots must eat quickly to replace the weight they lost during the winter and begin breeding as soon as possible to take advantage of the bountiful spring plant growth which they supplement with insects and birds' eggs.

Once the dominant female is pregnant she will take bedding material into the burrow before giving birth to a litter of around three to four babies. The babies are born blind, but within several days will have grown dark fur. In between bouts of suckling, the mother will come out to feed with the rest of the members of her colony, and the group often posts a sentry to watch out for predators such as golden eagles, while the rest of the animals have their heads down eating. As soon as they are weaned some 40 days later, the youngsters come out of the burrows to taste solid food for the first time, and it will then be a race against time to eat as much as possible before the temperature drops and hibernation beckons.

Being more vulnerable to the cold than their parents, it is crucial for the young Alpine marmots to eat a huge amount before the snow returns.

IN THE FAMILY WAY

As chimpanzees and humans were linked through a common ancestor a mere four to eight million years ago, it is no surprise that we share 98 per cent of our genetic blueprint with this great ape. Chimpanzees, or chimps, live in very complex communities, often comprising between 15 and 120 different individuals in the tropical forests and wet savannas of western and central Africa.

Chimps are equally happy on the ground, where they usually 'knuckle' walk on all fours, or in the trees, where they swing from branch to branch. They find most of their food in the trees and also choose to sleep there on leafy canopy platforms. Generally chimps eat fruit and plants but they have an incredibly varied diet which also includes insects, eggs and even meat if a monkey can be caught. They are one of the very few animals to employ tools, using specially-shaped sticks to dig grubs out of logs, or stones to break open tasty nuts.

Although the community may be large, chimps spend most of their time in small 'cliques' as they go about their daily business of grooming each other, feeding and travelling together. Females will mate with dominant males at any time of the year, and after an eight-month gestation period, they give birth to usually a single infant. The baby initially clings to its mother's fur, and when it is more confident it will ride on her back, but will still be totally reliant on her for food and protection for the next three years until weaned.

In spite of being closely related to us, these apes have suffered much by our hand, and while they are still hunted for bush-meat and their habitat is destroyed, they will continue to be one of our most endangered species, in addition to being our nearest cousin.

amily bonds are often
fe-long in the close-knit
orld of the chimpanzee.

OCEAN-GOING BABIES

Able to survive even in cold water, the leatherback is the world's largest living turtle and one of the animal world's great oceanic travellers. In common with all other sea turtles, the leatherback's flattened fore-limbs are extremely efficient aquatic flippers, but uniquely, the leatherback's bony shell is covered by a thick, leathery skin with a series of distinctive ridges running head to tail.

Weighing up to 800 kg (1,760 lb) in size and just a little under 2 m (6 ft 6 in) in length, the leatherback is able to hunt its favourite food – jellyfish – even in the cold waters of northern Europe and southern Africa. This is achieved because it can generate some of its own body heat, an extremely unusual feat amongst reptiles. Leatherbacks are normally found only in the open ocean, and the only time the adult females are ever seen on terra firma is when they briefly visit an ancestral tropical or sub-tropical beach to lay their eggs.

During a moonless night and after mating at sea, the pregnant females have two arduous tasks: first they have to haul their immense bulks up the beach using their flippers to propel them, and then they have to dig holes in the sand above the high-tide line, once again employing their multi-tooled flippers to excavate the ground. There they lay over a hundred eggs and cover them with sand before returning to the sea again. The turtle eggs hatch after 60 to 70 days and, under cover of darkness, the young hatchlings dig their way up to the surface, before making a dash *en masse* for the safety of the water and away from the beaks and teeth of numerous hungry predators.

With predation levels on the beach and in the sea so high only a tiny proportion of hatchlings will make it back to their birth site to breed as adults.

BABY BANDITS

Originating in the woodlands of North America, the raccoon has made such a success of living in towns and cities that in some cases it has become a real pest. The black facial markings of the raccoon additionally make it look just like a bandit, which is apt given its bold, opportunistic and thief-like habits.

With its black face and bushy black and white tail, the raccoon is a creature that cannot be confused with any other. Raccoons can either be active during the day or at night, and one of the keys to their success is their ability to eat almost anything from berries, insects and fruit, to small mammals, dog food and the trash from garbage bins. As they are so incredibly dextrous with their hands, they can easily manipulate the latches of doors and open discarded cans, too, and they also seem keen to show a high level of hygiene by rubbing off dirt and washing their ill-gotten gains in water before commencing dinner!

Although solitary, these animals may gather in numbers around plentiful food sources such as rubbish tips, but the only time that males and females spend any quality time together is when they meet briefly to mate in January or February. Unsurprisingly, males play no further part in the proceedings, and the litter of three to five young is born in a hollow tree, ground burrow, or under an outbuilding in April or May. The young will then spend the next two months being suckled safe and sound until they emerge in late summer, ready to try their luck in the neighbourhood.

Because of its supremely adaptable and resourceful nature, the raccoon has made a real success of living in North American cities.

MINI FLIPPERS

Famed for their ability to balance a ball on their noses in marine parks, sea lions can also be distinguished from their cousins, the seals, by the presence of small ears and the ability to rotate their back flippers forwards which makes movement on land easier. Of the six surviving species, the Japanese sea lion having already been made extinct, Hooker's sea lion is now the rarest.

Confined to a few small islands south of New Zealand, the total population of Hooker's sea lions is no more than around 12,000. When feeding the sea lions travel long distances offshore to forage for their favourite food of squid, octopus, crabs and fish. This can occasionally be supplemented by an unfortunate penguin if caught in the wrong place, at the wrong time!

Sea lions prefer sandy beaches for hauling out and will occasionally come well inland to rest amongst cliffs and trees in between foraging trips. Prior to the breeding season, the larger and darker males, or bulls, are the first to arrive on the beaches as they fight amongst themselves for a prime piece of 'sandy' real estate, before the pregnant females arrive a few weeks later. The single chocolate-coloured pups are born as soon as the mothers arrive and will immediately begin suckling on their incredibly rich milk. After mating with the dominant male, the mothers leave for sea but return every two or three days to feed their pups. Pups can swim after only a couple of weeks, but still rely on their mother's milk for the first year until they are ready to survive on their own four flippers.

It's sea lion milk for breakfast, lunch and dinner until the pup is finally ready to venture out to sea.

GOLDEN TWINS

With barely a thousand left in the wild, there are very few rarer monkeys than the highly threatened golden lion tamarins of Brazil's beleaguered Atlantic coastal forests. These engaging, alert little monkeys are aptly named due to the long, silky golden fur around their faces.

Reduced to the precipice of extinction by logging and resulting forest fragmentation, their homes consist of small territories amongst the dense tangle of vines, high in the forest canopy. The tamarins use these labyrinthine corridors to scamper around during their never-ending search for fruit, the occasional insect and rainwater concentrated in aerial bromeliad plants. The species forms small troops of up between five to fourteen individuals, consisting of a dominant mating pair, who are usually the only pair to rear young, and their offspring from previous breeding seasons.

Following a surprisingly long gestation period for such a small mammal of between 126 and 130 days, twins are quite commonly born to the leading female. After the birth, all the adult members of the troop are keen to help with babysitting, with the 'lion's' share of the duties surprisingly being carried out by the father, who adopts a very hands-on approach to his offspring. The youngsters become weaned by their mother at around 90 days, and if they can survive the perils of their first year, such as being eaten by birds of prey, cats or snakes, they may live for up to 15 years. Providing the tamarins' homes can be protected, and after a very successful captive breeding programme, there are hopes that the babies of these charming animals will continue to be reared in the tree-tops for many years to come.

e hair around golden lion marins' dark coloured ces cascades over their oulders in the manner a lion's mane.

MODEL OF MONOGAMY

This most regal of birds is instantly recognized by its dazzling white plumage, orange bill and gracefully curved neck. Originally from Europe and central Asia, the mute swan has been introduced to many parts of the world as an ornamental species. Nowhere is this swan more celebrated than in England, where the species is considered 'royal'; all unmarked birds have belonged to the Crown ever since the 'Act of Swans' was passed in 1482.

The Mute swan is one of the heaviest flying birds and larger males can reach an impressive 12 kg (26 lb). This weight means taking off can be a laborious process, involving an initial run and paddle across the water. Once airborne, however, they are powerful flyers, with their large wings making a distinctive whining sound as they pass overhead. The vast majority of pairs mate for life and, being creatures of habit, they will often use the same nesting location each year. The nest usually consists of a large mound built either close to the shore or floating on aquatic vegetation, and after an elaborate courtship which precedes the mating, a clutch of five to eight eggs will be laid.

The female swan incubates the eggs and it is the male or cob's job to protect the nest against any predators or intruding swans until the eggs hatch a month later, revealing ashy-grey coloured cygnets. When very young, the chicks will often hitch a ride on their parents' backs, but once their down is replaced by more mature brown feathers, they begin to copy their parents' upending technique to feed on the underwater plants. At the end of five months the young will be independent but still may not leave their parents' territory until they are driven away the following spring when their parents prepare to breed again.

'See no evil, hear no evil, speak no evil'... at least not whilst their father is around to protect them!

LITTLE BIG CATS

The 'top dog' of the African plains and savannas is ironically not canine but feline. Unlike all the other large cats, the lion's sexes can easily be distinguished: the much heavier males possess a large thick mane which they use for their own protection when fighting with and intimidating other lions.

The lion is by far the most sociable of all cats, banding together to form long-term social groups called prides. A pride consists of a group of around four to five related females, their cubs and a smaller number of unrelated males, who help the lionesses defend the area against other intruding lions enabling them to hold any mating rites.

In spite of being smaller, it is the quicker and lighter-footed lionesses that carry out the vast majority of the hunting. The pride operates in a well coordinated and effective team to ambush, chase and kill a variety of prey ranging from wildebeest and impala to even giraffe and elephant. Once the females have made a successful kill, the males will often then gate-crash to take their share of the spoils, having done little more than watch the spectacle from the sidelines!

All the lionesses in a pride will usually give birth at the same time, which means that the youngsters are able to suckle from any of the nursing mothers and can all be protected together. After being weaned at six months, life can be tough for the youngsters in the 'dog eat dog' world of the lions as they have to compete for food at dinner times.

Lion cubs are not quite natural born killers, but it doesn't take long to learn the hunting techniques necessary for survival.

BABY BROCKS

With its stocky build and uniquely marked black and white face, even those who have never seen a badger before will instantly recognize this most distinctive of nocturnal mammals. Found in a broad swathe across Europe and Asia, these very social beasts seem most at home in grazed pasture and woodland, where they can both dig to find enough food and also excavate the underground citadel in which they will spend a large proportion of their lives.

Badgers live in clans that vary in size between five and ten members, with a dominant male and female. Within the boundaries of their foraging territory, they will be the proud owners of an excavated network of tunnels and sleeping chambers called setts. During winter the more northerly badgers will spend most of their time in these setts in a deep sleep, only beginning to emerge regularly from early spring at dusk as they begin feeding again. Badgers eat virtually anything and will often vary their diet according to the season. Their favourite food is earthworms which they dig up with powerful paws and claws, but carrion, birds' eggs, bulbs and berries are also tracked down with a sense of smell 800 times more sensitive than humans!

Mating occurs in late winter or early spring, but because implantation of the eggs to the womb is delayed by ten months, the litter of up to six cubs is not born until the following January or February. The cubs are suckled by their mother for about ten weeks and in April they finally pluck up enough courage to leave the sanctuary of the sett and explore above ground. Where the movement is less restricted they adore indulging in a bit of rough and tumble with their siblings!

The world above ground mu
be a very exciting place for
baby badgers, having been
cooped up in the sett for the
first few months of their live

MALE MIDWIVES WANTED

Resembling a stunted common toad, the midwife toad is a decidedly unremarkable-looking toad who has, however, a remarkable method of breeding. Found across west and southwest Europe, with small populations surviving from accidental introductions in England, midwife toads are strictly nocturnal. Additionally, they do not congregate at breeding ponds, like most other frogs and toads, so they could best be described as inconspicuous for virtually the whole year!

During the day, midwife toads hide under logs, stones or in drystone walls, but they emerge at night between spring and autumn to search for food. They feed on a whole range of invertebrate prey, which they ensnare using their long, sticky tongues. Between April and June, and from the safety of their holes or burrows, the males call to any listening females with a distinctive and high-pitched 'poo-poo' call. Attracted by this call, any local females are invited to join the male in private, which results in the male climbing on the first arrival's back and holding on with a special grip called 'amplexus'. The female produces a set of large eggs, which are then fertilized by the male and promptly transferred to him before wrapping the sticky strings of eggs around his back and hind-limbs like a pearl necklace.

The eggs are carried around by the male midwife for between two and six weeks. Once the eggs are ready to hatch, the male moves to a suitable pond in which he sits whilst the tadpoles break free into the water.

The midwife toad has adopted a 'quality-not-quantity' approach to egg production.

STREETWISE YOUNGSTERS

Found right across North America, Europe, Asia, North Africa and Australia, the red fox is the most widespread wild carnivore in the world. Its resilient and adaptable nature also enables it to thrive in habitats ranging from the remote Arctic tundra to bustling city centres.

The fox can be remarkably unfussy when it comes to food and almost anything edible is generally considered fair game. In addition to eating worms, beetles and eggs, rural foxes are more likely to catch rabbits and hares, whilst their urban cousins consume a higher proportion of carrion and human refuse.

The fox's home is usually in a sheltered spot such as an old animal burrow, or under an outbuilding, with each animal claiming its own territory until it pairs up to share resources in preparation for winter breeding. The male fox (dog) and the female (vixen) will mark their joint territory with urine and droppings and keep in contact with a combination of nocturnal yapping calls and blood-curdling screams. Mating occurs in late winter or early spring, with the litter of between five and eight cubs being born around 50 days later in an underground 'maternity' den or earth.

Born blind, naked and helpless, the cubs are suckled by the vixen, but will not take their first tentative steps above ground for at least five weeks. At this stage, the youngsters are incredibly playful with each other, as they begin to learn the vital skills they will eventually need to survive when they disperse to claim their own territories.

Due to the catholic nature of a fox's diet, this begging youngster will never know what to expect for dinner!

LIFE IN THE SLOW LANE

While a koala is a 'must-see' for anyone visiting the coastal forests of eastern and southern Australia, it has to be said that as apparently cuddly as it is, the koala is not the most exciting creature to watch. Spending almost its entire life high up in the canopy of eucalyptus trees, koalas enjoy a life 'in the slow lane', as they spend anywhere between 18 and 20 hours a day wedged asleep in the fork of a branch!

When not dozing, koalas pass the rest of their time munching up to 500 g (1 lb 2 oz) of eucalyptus leaves each at night. These leaves are low in protein, highly indigestible and full of toxic compounds. Digestion of this material is aided by effective bacterial fermentation in their guts, with the toxins being deactivated by a specially enlarged liver.

Despite the koala generally being a silent animal, the loud advertising calls of the males can be heard over large distances during the breeding season. The dominant males mate with most of the females and the resulting pregnancy is brief: the baby koala or 'joey' is born naked, hairless and barely 7 or 8 mm (1/3 in) in length. The tiny maggot-like newborn then crawls into the downward-facing pouch, where it fastens onto one of the two teats. Nothing is then seen of the youngster for the next six months as it develops ears, eyes and fur on a diet of pure koala milk.

After it emerges from the pouch, the joey will spend another six months with its mother before becoming fully independent. One of the joey's first meals consists of its mother's droppings; these contain an ample supply of food-digesting microbes, and it is these which help the youngster convert the unpalatable and almost indigestible leaves into a tasty midnight snack.

Not until it is six months old does the joey put in an appearance, as it finally plucks up the courage to leave its mother's pouch.

BORN SPOTTY

The fallow deer originates in the Middle East and parts of the Mediterranean and an ability to be easily tamed has led to its introduction to deer parks across an array of countries beyond their natural range. Although their coats can be variable, the most common colour of this handsome deer is pale brown flecked by large white mottles. Apart from a short period between spring and early summer, when the old antlers have been shed and new sets are still to form, the males, or bucks, can easily be distinguished by their broad shovel-shaped antlers. This head-gear will prove vital later in the year as they fight for the right to mate.

The bucks will spend most of the year roaming away from the herds of females, or does, and their young. Irrespective of sex, deer are generally most active at dawn and dusk as they graze on grasses, ground plants, and shrubs; the rest of the time they lie up and quietly chew the cud in the undergrowth.

The mating, or rut, takes place in the autumn. All the deer come together and the biggest stags, by a combination of posturing, bellowing and fighting (when necessary), assert their dominance as they herd the does into their respective territories for mating. After about 230 days, a single spotted fawn is born in the long grass and for the first week or two of its life it remains perfectly still, silent and camouflaged from predators, only moving when its mother returns to suckle it. Only when stronger will a fawn be able to leave its hiding place for good and be free to frolic with the herd.

With so many predators around, it pays for a fallow fawn to be spotty, camouflaged and silent for the first couple of weeks of life.

THE LONGEST JOURNEY

Confined to the remote outposts of Australia, kangaroos are instantly recognizable beasts. With their clown-like hind limbs, seemingly useless forelimbs and prop-like tail, they resemble oddly-shaped giant rabbits as they gently browse on grasses and leafy shrubs. However, when in a hurry, they transform into animals of great power and athletic grace, as their mighty back legs propel them along in a bizarre but highly effective hopping style that can reach speeds of up to 50 km/h (31 mph).

Like other mammals, the female gives birth to live young, but as kangaroos belong to a specialized and ancient sub-group called the marsupials, their babies enter into the world at a very early stage of life. At birth the grey kangaroo youngster weighs less than 1 g (1/25 oz) and upon being born, this animated kidney bean has to make an incredible voyage across its mother's fur to reach the safety of the pouch where, upon arrival, it attaches itself to one of the four nipples on offer. The tiny youngster will then remain firmly fastened to the teat for the next 130 to 150 days as it grows quickly on its mother's milk. Only after 250 days will the young kangaroo or 'joey' finally feel brave enough to leave the security blanket of its mother's pouch as it pops out for short exploratory periods, before diving back in at the remotest sign of danger.

In many kangaroo species the female will mate again whilst pregnant, but the new embryo remains dormant and will not embark on its marathon journey until its elder sibling is finally ejected out of the pouch for good!

ven when far too large for
s mother's pouch, the
oung grey kangaroo will
till try to clamber back
 if scared.

ALL FOR ONE
AND ONE FOR ALL

With a coat consisting of irregular swirls of black, yellow and white fur, it is perhaps apt that this most sociable of all the wild dogs is frequently also called 'the painted wolf'.

In its strongholds of the game reserves in eastern and southern Africa, the African wild dog lives in large packs of up to 30 closely-related adults and young. Each pack contains a dominant male and female and only this pair is permitted to breed. The raising of the litter is, however, a family affair, as the whole pack pulls together to protect and care for the young, until they have developed the bulk, speed and other necessary skills to run with the pack and join in the hunt.

Packs of African wild dogs often register top success rates – as high as 80 per cent – when chasing down their chosen prey of impala, zebra and even wildebeest. Their technique involves teamwork as they pursue their prey for long distances, often at speeds of up to 70 km/h (43 mph). As the dogs then close in on their unfortunate target, they communicate through a series of chirping whistles to ensure a successful kill.

In an abandoned underground den dug by animals such as aardvarks, the dominant female will produce a large litter of ten to twelve pups. After feeding on their mother's milk for the first ten weeks, both they and the alpha female are fed regurgitated meat by other faithful family members returning from victorious hunts. By the age of three months, the playful cubs will be able to follow the adults and their elder siblings on hunts, but they will still need a further nine months to perfect the fine art of coordinated killing.

All the packs pull together t ensure the young cubs have enough food to eat until the are able to run with the pac

BORN TO BOX

Unlike its cousin the rabbit, which digs to escape beyond the reach of predators, the brown or European hare is an animal that spends its entire life above ground. However, instead of being able to dive into bolt-holes for protection, the hare has been blessed with fleetness of foot and the agility to turn on a sixpence, which means it can easily outrun most dangers.

Hares are usually fairly solitary animals. During the day they quietly rest up in shallow depressions called 'forms', and only become more active at dusk when they emerge to feed on a variety of grasses and crops. In early spring, as the breeding season approaches, the hares' behaviour changes and they become more sociable and energetic in the daytime. The animals can be seen chasing each other around the fields, as the male hares try to assert dominance over the other males, and the larger females 'box' away any unwanted attention from over-amorous males.

Eventually the most dominant male will manage to break down the female's resistance, and after a pregnancy of around 40 days, three to five leverets are born fully furred and with their eyes open. Almost immediately the leverets will then move away from the birth-site and hide. By splitting up into different 'forms', they minimize the risk of the whole litter being uncovered together by their arch enemy, the fox. Following sunset, the mother will very briefly visit each of her leverets to suckle them in turn. After a month they are ready to move onto solids and will begin a life of nibbling.

Unable to escape underground, the leverets must initially rely on camouflage until they have developed the speed to outrun any danger.

JUNIOR KINGS
OF THE JUNGLE

As a result of habitat destruction, fragmentation and hunting, the tiger population has been reduced to just pockets of forest in southern and eastern Asia. However, in locations where sufficient habitat and prey are present and the tiger is left in peace, he is still very much 'king of the jungle'.

Unlike his African counterparts – the lion and cheetah – which hunt in open habitats, the tiger is very much a 'stalk and ambush' predator which is most effective when hunting alone. It is thought that the pattern of stripes, which are unique to each individual animal, serves as perfect camouflage to keep the tiger hidden before he bursts from cover to catch and then overpower his chosen quarry.

Tigers pass much of their lives in a solitary fashion, but they are not necessarily antisocial, and females in adjoining territories occasionally meet up. The local male will be invited to join a receptive female by the chemical messages she leaves in her scent markings, which indicate her willingness to mate. After a pregnancy lasting just over 100 days, two or three blind and helpless cubs, weighing no more than 1 kg (2 lb 3 oz), are born. For the first two months they will be confined to the den site and a diet of their mother's milk, but after this they will begin to follow her lead with their first tentative steps.

Now that this charismatic animal is threatened in most of its native countries and faces much adversity, let us hope that the tiger, to paraphrase the poet William Blake, continues to 'burn bright'.

Whilst the tiger cubs are independent at around 18 months, they will still rely on their surprisingly tender mother before they are ready to face the jungle on their own.

SLOWLY DOES IT

The sloth is one of the most successful and abundant of all the large animals that live in the tropical forests of Central and South America. Vilified because of its name, it is perhaps unjust to demonize this misunderstood creature just because of its lazy lifestyle. Of the six species of sloth, the most common is the brown-throated, three-toed sloth.

Sloths are about the size of a small dog, and have small heads, tiny eyes and hidden ears, which contrast with their large body and powerful limbs. The coarse, outer coat of fur is particularly long around their head, neck and shoulders and, as befits their generally inactive lifestyle, usually becomes colonized by algae, mites, ticks and even moths! Sloths feed almost exclusively on leaves and have a special multi-chambered stomach to enable them to ferment this tough vegetable matter. They only come down to the ground if they need to either defecate, or to move on to another tree if it is not possible to travel though the branches.

During the mating season, the solitary females attract the males with a loud human-like scream, and after a pregnancy lasting five to six months, the single newborn baby sloth immediately clings to its mother's belly with a set of well-developed grappling hooks. The youngster is weaned after a month, but will still be carried around by its mother for another six months while it learns how, where and what to eat. Protected by their camouflaged coat and a remarkable ability to freeze for hours, they appear to have comparatively few predators and in the wild they can live for over twelve years.

The baby three-toed sloth will cling to its mother's belly for at least the first seven months of life before a long, slow and possibly emotional separation.

A LONG AND
FRUITFUL LIFE

Confined to the famed Galápagos archipelago, the Galápagos giant tortoise holds the distinction of being the largest living tortoise. With a number of different subspecies dotted across the different isles, the heaviest males can weigh over 300 kg (661 lb), and are believed to reach the unbelievable age of more than 150 years. The most distinguishing feature of the Galápagos tortoises is their shell; this is composed of bone and is fused inside with their ribs to form a protective shield into which they can withdraw if perturbed.

Adult tortoises have no natural predator and acquire their enormous size and immense longevity just on a vegetarian diet of cactus, grass, leaves and fruit. Their days are spent either basking in the sun to warm up, grazing in small, peaceful herds or sleeping in mud wallows. During the breeding season the larger males become territorial, and rely on a fairly brutal courtship technique, which entails them using their huge shell to ram the smaller female into submission. The male tortoise then nips at her legs to immobilize her, leaving him free to clamber onto her shell so that mating can take place.

The female will then dig a trench in dry, sandy ground and lay between two and sixteen eggs before covering them over. Upon hatching, the tiny tortoises then dig their way up to the surface before embarking on a long and fruitful life.

Whilst able to reproduce after around 25 years, it is not until 40 years of age that a baby tortoise will have finally reached full size.

A NEW AGE
RELATIONSHIP

Seahorses are surely one of the most bizarre-looking groups of animals in the natural world. It is not surprising that the Latin name for seahorses is *Hippocampus*: this is a direct translation of the words for a horse and a caterpillar – and seahorses really do look like a cross between the two!

There are around 35 known species of seahorse and all their babies are the product of a very loving yet unconventional relationship. Monogamy is the lifestyle of choice for these wonderful creatures: they are so devoted to each other that if one of them dies the surviving partner will often go through a period of grieving. Every morning the pair meet up to perform an elaborate courtship display and in doing so they reaffirm their commitment to one another.

It is, however, their love-life which is truly amazing, with the only known reversed pregnancy in the natural world. The male is the ultimate 'new-age dad', as he is the one who actually gives birth to the young, a role he takes very seriously. After external fertilization, the male's chosen life partner deposits her eggs through an ovipositor into his special brood pouch. The male then incubates the young for up to a month before undergoing a protracted period of labour which results in the ejection of around 1,000 tiny, yet perfect replicas of their parents over a period of twelve hours.

With so many predators in the ocean, the baby that survives to adulthood and its wedding vows will be literally one in a thousand.

A CUCKOO IN THE NEST

The call of the male cuckoo is considered the quintessential sound of spring, but it is merely the first step in a chick-rearing process that is so audacious as to be scarcely believable.

To say the parents' contribution to bringing up their chick is minimal would be a huge understatement. Once the male cuckoo has mated as many females as possible, it is 'job done' as far as he is concerned, and he starts the long trip from northern Europe back to Africa. The female, however, must find a host-nest in which to place her own egg to be brought up by the unsuspecting parents of another species. Reed warblers, meadow pipits and dunnocks are the favourite quarry for the female cuckoo as she painstakingly searches for a nest with a temporarily unguarded clutch of eggs.

Once located, she swoops in, removing a host egg and replacing it with one of her own, which often is a remarkable replica. The cuckoo's egg quickly hatches and the newborn chick then performs the miraculous yet heinous feat of ejecting the host birds' own eggs and chicks out of the nest. This then leaves the little parasite as the sole recipient of all of the food brought back to the nest by the totally unsuspecting hosts.

With such undivided attention, the chick soon looks preposterously huge next to its foster parents, which quite often have to stand on the chick's back to reach its gaping mouth. Once the chick has successfully fledged, the juvenile cuckoo will leave its breeding ground to cross the Sahara Desert *en route* to a warm winter south of the Equator.

Totally unaware that it has been duped, this reed warbler will continue to forage dawn to dusk until the thankless cuckoo chick has fledged.

BABIES FROM MARS

Resembling a cross between an over-sized rodent and a monkey it is no surprise that the only place that the bizarre aye-aye can be found is on the weird and wonderful island of Madagascar. Separated from the main continent of Africa for millions of years, the world's fourth largest island houses a unique mix of animals, which have evolved in isolation and, in many cases, look very different from their continental cousins.

While combining the body of a monkey with a bushy squirrel-like tail, the aye-aye's face is actually pointed like a raccoon. In addition, it has large incisors which grow continuously throughout its lifetime and a distinctive pair of luminous eyes. Without doubt the aye-aye's most unusual feature, however, is its slender middle finger which is three times longer than all its other digits and is used to extract grubs out of holes made by its sharp teeth. This makes the aye-aye the Madagascan equivalent of a nocturnal woodpecker!

At around sunset the aye-aye emerges from its bird-like stick nest in the canopy. This primitive and mostly solitary monkey can cover large distances as it leaps around the canopy like a squirrel, hunting for fruits, nuts and seeds and in addition to its favourite juicy grubs.

By leaving regular scent marks across their home ranges, the females are able to let the males know when they are ready to mate, and the successful male will then stay close by until the baby is born some five months later. The youngster is weaned after seven months, and while it occasionally shares food with its father, it will rely mostly on its mother, who also indulges the baby with wrestling, chasing and 'peek-a-boo' games for a further two years.

alf monkey, half rodent and
ving in a nest... it can only
e a baby aye-aye.

KILLER BABIES

The distinctive black-and-white markings and tall dorsal fin of the killer whale, or orca, make this the most easily recognized of all the toothed whales and dolphins. This highly social whale is also one of the most powerful predators and versatile hunters of the sea, as they cooperate together to feast on a variety of prey ranging from seals and squid to seabirds and even other whale species.

Although they more commonly frequent cold, coastal waters, orcas are a truly cosmopolitan species, and can be found anywhere from the polar region to the tropics. The whales live in long-lasting family pods of up to 30 individuals, which consist of males, females and calves of different ages. These pods tend to be led by a dominant female, and as both male and female calves stay with their mother for life, this can result in as many as four generations of the same family surrounding a maternal figurehead. The adult females only produce calves every five years after a long pregnancy of 15 to 18 months, and although the young stay closest to their mothers until weaned, the whole pod will be ready to swim in close and provide parental care when necessary.

Some of the orca pods tend to be resident, while other groups seem to lead a more nomadic existence. Despite this all the members will stay in constant communication with each other as they hunt. There seems to be plenty of time for the extended family to socialize too, and they will often indulge in breaching, spy-hopping (where they pop their heads up like a periscope), and also slapping their flukes on the water, when they feel the need to burn off any excess energy!

Looking more softie than killer, killer whale calves will keep incredibly strong bonds with their mothers throughout their lives.

FURRY DUCKLINGS

With its duck-like bill, beaver tail, dense fur and webbed feet, the platypus is indeed a very odd-looking animal. So when a specimen first arrived in Britain, it is not surprising that naturalists thought it was an elaborate hoax. While it is genuine of course, the platypus does still continue to beggar belief, as it has the distinction of being only one of two mammals to lay eggs, instead of giving birth to live young.

The platypus spends at least twelve hours a day foraging in the small streams and rivers of its native eastern Australia and Tasmania. Generally nocturnal, this excellent swimmer uses its highly specialized bill to dig into the bottoms of stream in order to detect the electrical signals emitted from the moving muscles of its prey, such as insect larvae, freshwater shrimps and crayfish.

Whilst platypuses are solitary, they have overlapping home ranges which are stoutly defended by the males during the breeding season. The male possesses a poisonous spur on each hind-foot, which, it is thought, he uses as a weapon to wound any rival males intent on taking over his territory. After mating, the female will construct a deep burrow of up to 20 m (66 ft) in length, before filling the end with nesting material and laying two to three grape-sized eggs. The female will then curl around the eggs to incubate them until they hatch, after which the blind, naked platypus babies will be fed on their mother's milk, which is delivered not through teats, but pores in the skin. After three to four months of suckling, these bizarre-looking youngsters will be ready to leave the burrow and finally forage for themselves.

ooking like the missing
nk between birds and
ammals, young platypuses
re ready to make it on
eir own after just three
o four months.

NATURAL BORN SYMBOL

The immense and powerful bald eagle is recognized throughout the world as the national bird of the United States of America. So-called because of its gleaming white-feathered head, which matches the white tail, yet contrasts with the brown body plumage, the bald eagle is the only native eagle to be found solely in North America.

With a wingspan of nearly 2.5 m (8 ft 2 in) and weighing up to 6 kg (13 lb), the bald eagle also has size and brawn to back up its brazen good looks. Most of their year is spent close to lakes, rivers and the coast, which gives them ample access to fish which they snatch from the water with powerful talons. Carrion and small mammals also feature in their diet, and they will even resort to stealing other predators' meals when opportunities prevail. During the breeding season they also need tall, mature stands of trees in which they are able to breed, making them masters of all they survey!

The bald eagle's nest is actually the largest nest of any North American bird. Breeding pairs usually mate at the same location for life, and by adding sticks incrementally each season the nest can reach impressive dimensions of 4 m (13 ft) in depth, 2 m (6 ft 7 in) across and a weight of close to a tonne. Whilst a normal bald eagle clutch varies from one to three eggs, it is rare for all three chicks to successfully fledge. Despite their parents' best efforts, both eggs and chicks can be taken by other birds, and any shortage of food during the breeding season will often mean that only the biggest chick will survive.

With these three chicks looking healthy and ready to fledge, it has obviously been a good season's hunting for the parents.

INDEX

PICTURE CREDITS

ACKNOWLEDGEMENTS

At HarperCollins I would like to thank Myles Archibald, Julia Koppitz and Heike Schüssler for making writing my second full book such an enjoyable, fun and straightforward process.

Thanks also to my partner Christina for being so patient, and to my mum Renee, brothers Paul and Andy and their partners and families for being so supportive and encouraging.

Finally thanks to my dear pals Ed Miller, Mark Flowers and Ed Drewitt for proving there is life beyond work sometimes!